WOMEN IN ACTION
Rebels and Reformers, 1920-1980

Elisabeth Israels Perry

Women in Action: Rebels and Reformers 1920-1980 is a public education project of the League of Women Voters Education Fund that addresses the relationships between women's activism and grassroots politics during the post-suffrage era. It celebrates the 75th anniversary of the 19th Amendment as well as the 75th anniversary of the League of Women Voters. The project is comprised of three components: a national exhibit, which will travel the United States in 1995-96, this companion publication and a series of scholarly presentations at exhibit sites. Funding is provided by a grant from the National Endowment for the Humanities. Call the League of Women Voters Education Fund (202-429-1965) for more information.

Curator
Priscilla Rachun Linn, D. Phil

Publication Author
Elisabeth Israels Perry, Ph.D

Exhibition and Publication Design
Chester Design Associates, Inc.

League of Women Voters Education Fund
Becky Cain, Chair
Carole Wagner Vallianos, Project Trustee
Kathleen Weisenberg, Project Trustee
Nancy Di Giulian, Program Manager

©1995 League of Women Voters Education Fund

Pub. #1019, $6.95 ($5.95 for members), plus $2.00 shipping and handling.
Quantity discounts on request.
Printed on recycled paper.

ISBN 0-89959-389-5

Order from Publications Sales,
League of Women Voters,
1730 M Street, NW,
Washington, DC 20036.

Phone 202-429-1965. Fax 202-429-0854.

Contents

CHAPTER ONE
The Place of Women in American Political History   **1**

CHAPTER TWO
Women's Social Welfare Movements after Suffrage   **9**

CHAPTER THREE
Rights for Women   **19**

CHAPTER FOUR
Women in the Civil Rights Movement   **29**

CHAPTER FIVE
Labor and the Economy   **39**

CHAPTER SIX
Women in Peace Activism and International Affairs   **49**

CONCLUSION
Does Women's Participation Count?   **56**

CHAPTER ONE

THE PLACE OF WOMEN IN AMERICAN POLITICAL HISTORY

American women always have been political, even when they were excluded from party membership, voting and running for office. They took sides on political issues and participated in party activities. Women in the western territories and states were voting long before the national woman suffrage amendment of 1920. By 1904, 20 states allowed women to vote for school boards; in other states and municipalities, women voted on tax measures. By 1913, ten states had given women the franchise.

Even before women had the vote in any state, they were influencing the outcome of political controversies. Prominent women influenced powerful men directly, but most women worked through voluntary associations. Although some women joined mixed-sex groups, such as the early temperance societies, more joined single-sex organizations, such as the female antislavery societies founded in the 1830s. Membership in single-sex groups gave women greater access to leadership roles and more control over their programs for action.

Women with neither the time nor the opportunity to join an organized society used more spontaneous means of political expression. They protested, picketed and took part in crowd actions when circumstances—such as wage cuts during periods of economic depression, or food shortages and price gouging during wartime—pushed them to the edge of patience or desperation. Sometimes, striking or demonstrating women formed organizations, but these were usually short-lived. Even so, women's spontaneous political actions comprise an important feature of women's political history before suffrage.

Until quite recently, historians of American political life gave little attention to women's political activism, organized *or* spontaneous. They not only downplayed the importance of woman suffrage but also of women's political roles since suffrage. Today's historians are challenging versions of the American past in which women fail to appear as significant actors. The purpose of *Women in Action: Rebels and Reformers 1920-1980* is to introduce this ongoing reexamination of the historical record.

Woman Suffrage: A Dream of Full Citizenship

By the second decade of the twentieth century, hundreds of thousands of American women, representing different social classes, races and ethnic origins had joined the movement for woman suffrage, a struggle that had been going on since 1848. Even after years of frustration and disappointment, suffragists were still committed to their goal. What made them so determined?

Critics accused them of wanting the vote in order to overturn the social order, elevating women above men or, worse, allowing women to act as if they *were* men. In fact, most women wanted the vote because it meant full citizenship, a status denied them since the founding of the republic. In addition, many suffragists were convinced that the vote would lead to an end to male control over women's earnings, careers, property and offspring. Equally important, the vote was a means to a direct exercise of power. Much in society needed fixing. Because women lacked the vote, political men had kept them on the margins when they sought to steer the direction of change, or had ignored them altogether.

The first political cause to attract early nineteenth-century American women in substantial numbers was the abolition of slavery. Despite an international revulsion against slavery that had been rising since the late eighteenth century, African Americans continued to be worked, whipped and abused with impunity in the United States. The abolitionist movement included hundreds of white women and free black women, their abhorrence of slavery deepening their anger over their own political powerlessness.

Concerns about "vice" also drew women into political activism. Realizing that gambling, prostitution and drinking impoverished and destroyed families, women by the thousands waged anti-vice campaigns across the country. "Purity" and "temperance" campaigns began as efforts to save individuals who either gave in to vice or were its victims. The campaigns later sought to control vice through government regulation or outright prohibition.

Women also were horrified by the treatment of the insane as criminals, the adulteration of food and drugs, the crowding of urban immigrants into substandard housing and the increasingly exploitative, unsafe conditions in American factories. Such issues captured women's imaginations in the presuffrage years and drew them into political movements for change.

Most women's voluntary associations started out in local communities and were directed toward religious or benevolent ends. Societies committed to moral reform often spread to larger arenas. Their members organized fairs and bazaars to raise money, wrote newsletters and newspapers, kept up a relentless correspondence with one another and with officials, gathered and presented petitions for action, and sent delegations to legislators and officials. They organized public meetings and addressed them, even though public speech-making breached nineteenth-century conventions for proper womanly behavior, especially when the audience included both women and men.

Flouting convention even further, nineteenth-century women carried petitions door-to-door, testified before legislative bodies, and pleaded with and harried public officials. Despite misgivings about the excessive interest of politicians in the spoils of office, some women took part in political party campaigns. Others engaged in more radical efforts, such as organizing boycotts of goods made by slave labor. Temperance and purity campaigners publicized the names of the "solid citizens" whose investments and patronage supported saloons, gambling houses and brothels. Suffragists disrupted public meetings and engaged in civil disobedience. Arguing that suffrage was an inalienable right of citizenship under the Fourteenth Amendment, they

"We do not consider ourselves subject to this court, since as an unenfranchised class we have nothing to do with the making of the laws which have put us in this position."

—Alice Paul

> *"I propose a League of Women Voters, nonpartisan and non-sectarian, to finish the fight and to aid in the reconstruction of the nation. What should be done can be done; what can be done, let us do."*
>
> —Carrie Chapman Catt

attempted to vote even when threatened with arrest for doing so.

Action groups usually have been constructed along homogeneous lines. At times, women united "as women" to achieve specific goals, or built cross-class, cross-ethnic and interracial alliances. Generally, however, just as men did, women excluded women unlike themselves, even those they claimed to be most interested in helping. Some white abolitionist, temperance and suffrage organizations invited African American women to participate but then neglected their concerns or treated them condescendingly. Frustrated by their experience in integrated groups, African American women founded their own societies. These went on to play central roles in the anti-segregation and anti-lynching movements of the early twentieth century.

Some of women's presuffrage campaigns were stunningly successful. Prohibition of the sale and manufacture of alcoholic beverages, legislated at first on local levels, eventually took on national proportions. Congress passed national prohibition with the Eighteenth Amendment in 1918, in part as a war measure but also as a result of intense public pressure created by the Woman's Christian Temperance Union and other groups. Ultimately, because prohibition led to more anti-social and criminal behavior than it prevented, the nation declared it a failure and repealed it with the Twenty-First Amendment in 1933. It remains a local option in some counties.

Women's groups campaigned to pass laws to regulate tenements, fund efforts in public housing and public health, and inspect factories. Women social reformers led the movement to establish a new federal agency, the Children's Bureau (1912), which investigated the conditions of child labor and fostered protections for the country's children. Ironically, the success of women's reform campaigns prompted anti-suffragists to argue that women hardly needed the vote to be politically effective.

By the early twentieth century, however, suffrage had gained wide public appeal. Ratified at long last in August 1920, the Nineteenth Amendment to the Constitution had required a tremendous political effort from women of all ethnic groups and races. Suffrage leader Carrie Chapman Catt counted "fifty-six campaigns of referenda to male voters; 480 campaigns to get Legislatures to submit suffrage amendments to voters; 47 campaigns to get State constitutional conventions to write woman suffrage into state constitutions; 277 campaigns to get State party conventions to include woman suffrage planks; 30 campaigns to get presidential party conventions to adopt woman suffrage planks in party platforms, and 19 campaigns with 19 successive Congresses."

Since Catt disapproved of what militant suffragists had done in order to win the vote, she omitted their actions in her summary. Militants had campaigned against Democratic party congressional candidates because the national party had not endorsed woman suffrage. They demonstrated in front of the White House, burning copies of President Wilson's speeches and even his effigy. For the "crime" of blocking traffic while demonstrating, the militants were jailed. When they went on hunger strikes to protest the conditions of their imprisonment, they were forcibly fed by painful and damaging means. Horror at their treatment helped turn the tide of national public opinion toward suffrage.

A Dream Unfulfilled?

Many historians have argued that giving women the vote changed little on the larger American political landscape. In the early years after suffrage, fewer women than expected actually voted, and when they did, their votes reflected political differences similar to those among men. While these observations are true, they need to be placed in a broader picture.

The number of voting women may have been low because voter interest in general had declined since the turn of the twentieth century; it fell even further in the 1920s. Moreover, politics intimidated many ordinary women. Some older women claimed ignorance of the issues. Others feared their husbands' disapproval. Although some younger women valued the vote as a symbol of new freedoms, many of them were more interested in personal than political pursuits. And finally, poll taxes and literacy tests disfranchised many potential new voters, including African Americans and the poor.

Woman suffrage did make a difference in some local elections. At community and state levels, women voters often supported or opposed candidates for reasons related to women's causes. As Edna Kenton pointed out in her article "Four Years of Equal Suffrage" (*The Forum*, July 1924), "a debatable candidate for a purely local office is likely to be less certain of election now than in the good old days when the gang gathered to vote and the respectable citizen stayed disgustedly at home." Moreover, the success of women's policy agendas, some of which are described in this publication, would not have occurred without women's enfranchisement.

Equally important, the vote gave individual women access to political posts that they otherwise would not have had. In 1920, the Democratic National Committee asked every state to elect a committeewoman as well as a committeeman; in 1924, the Republican National Committee followed suit. As a result, political women rose at state levels. Among them were Nellie Nugent Somerville in Mississippi, Sue Shelton White in Tennessee, Emily Newell Blair in Missouri, Edna Frohmiller in Arizona, Nellie Tayloe Ross in Wyoming, Florence Fifer Bohrer and Ruth Hanna McCormick in Illinois, Cornelia Bryce Pinchot and Emma Guffey Miller in Pennsylvania, and Belle Moskowitz and Eleanor Roosevelt in New York. Several women won election to Congress, and two women succeeded their husbands as governors. By 1929, 149 women were serving in state legislatures in 38 states; by 1931, only Louisiana lacked a female legislator.

Still, progress was slow. Political parties remained male-dominated. Most of the women who won major elective office were related by

---

THE NINETEENTH AMENDMENT TO THE CONSTITUTION OF THE UNITED STATES

The right of citizens of the United States to vote shall not be denied or abridged by the United States or by any State on account of sex.

Congress shall have power to enforce this article by appropriate legislation.

birth or marriage to important political men; their election relied heavily on voter recognition of their prominent names, even though many of them had been active suffragists.

After suffrage, most political women continued to work behind the scenes, becoming, for example, leaders of the parties' women's divisions or committees. As more women earned advanced degrees, especially in the fields of law, social science and public administration, a few earned important party and government offices. Some began to play advisory roles to powerful party men. By the 1930s and 1940s, women attorneys and judges began to influence the terms of reform legislation, ensure its enforcement and defend its constitutionality.

The vast majority of women political activists continued to work as they had in the past, through nonpartisan voluntary associations. Although they joined mixed-sex groups, most women still felt more comfortable in single-sex groups, such as the League of Women Voters (LWV), the successor organization to the National American Woman Suffrage Association, or the numerous women's civic organizations already active in cities across the country. The political agendas of these organizations varied. Some concentrated on one cause. Most worked across a range of related causes, such as social welfare, women's rights, civil rights, labor reform and peace. Some groups lasted only a few years and had primarily local significance; others grew into national organizations that endure to this day.

Over the decades after suffrage, women's organizations trained large numbers of women for local and national leadership and influenced the development of public policies at all government levels. The most prominent women's organizations for a long time consisted primarily of native-born, middle- to upper-class women of European American origins. Women representing these mainstream groups therefore dominate the story of women's political activism in the modern era. As historians uncover more of the activities of women of various income levels and ethnic and racial backgrounds, American women's political history will continue to be rewritten.

CHAPTER TWO

Women's Social Welfare Movements After Suffrage

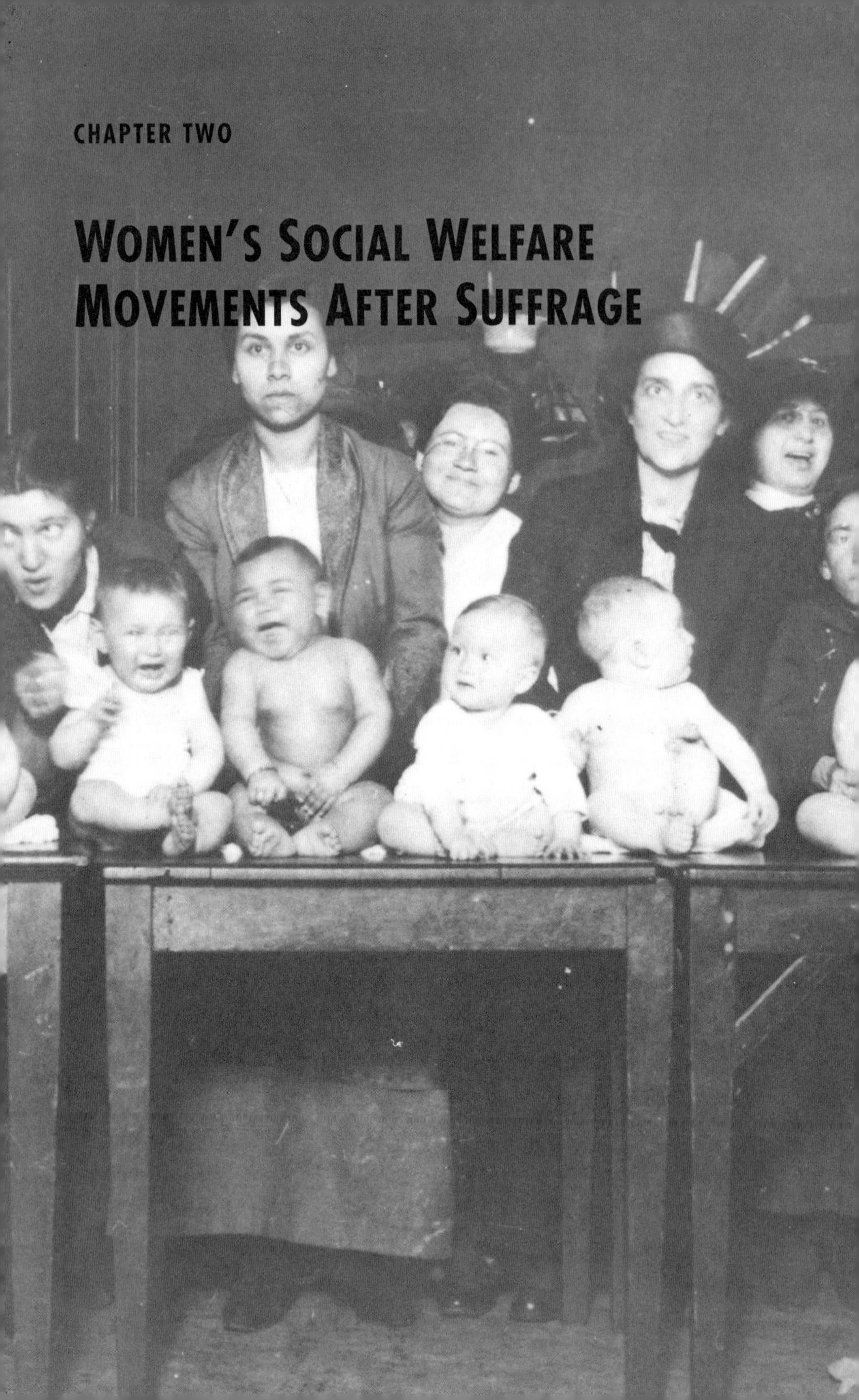

Before winning the vote, American suffragists had long been concerned with those in society unable to care for themselves. Beginning around the 1890s, at the start of the period historians call the Progressive Era, middle-class women disturbed by the widening gap between America's social classes began to articulate new ideas about the role of the state. In their view, the state should do more than just govern. It should help people in need and protect the weak. Referring to this kind of state as a "maternal commonwealth," suffragists believed that the woman's vote would bring it about.

Working in the Community

The experience of social settlement workers, large numbers of whom were college-educated women, lay at the basis of these ideas. Settlement work began in this country in the late 1880s. Jane Addams and Ellen Gates Starr were two of its most famous practitioners. In the belief that charity, dispensed either in money or services from the top down, rarely helped the poor, Addams and Starr decided to live in a poor neighborhood to find out how they could help. They bought the dilapidated Charles Hull mansion in Chicago, renovated it and opened its doors to their immigrant neighbors.

After settling in, Addams and Starr developed programs and services in response to community needs. They set up child care centers, clubs for children and young adults, playgrounds and roof gardens, employment and legal aid bureaus, and health care clinics. Their work soon made them aware of the growing need for better city services and other reforms. To achieve reform, they investigated social and political conditions and then pressured officials for change.

By 1910, there were more than 400 settlement houses in American cities. Throughout the following decade, thousands of settlement workers campaigned for social reforms as well as woman suffrage. After suffrage was won in 1920, they helped form networks of reformers to set priorities and plan strategies. Their goals included better working conditions for women (a shorter work week, rest periods and welfare programs), the curbing of child labor, improved prison systems and better services for the poor. Despite political hostility to these goals in the 1920s, women's voluntary organizations continued to work for them. Most prominent were the General Federation of Women's

Clubs, the Young Women's Christian Association, the Council of Jewish Women, the National Association of Colored Women, the Women's Trade Union League, the National Consumers' League, the National Federation of Business and Professional Women, and the League of Women Voters.

Working Through Government

The first item on the welfare agenda for postsuffrage women was to lower infant and maternal mortality rates that at the time were higher in the United States than in most industrialized countries. Working through the Children's Bureau, reformers proposed that public health nurses educate women in prenatal care and early childhood nutrition, sanitation and child care. Spearheaded by the League of Women Voters, representatives from ten other women's organizations created a Women's Joint Congressional Committee, which in November 1921 achieved passage of the Sheppard-Towner Maternity and Infancy Protection Act by Congress.

Getting the legislation passed and ensuring its enforcement were not easy. Industrial reformer and National Consumers' League (NCL) head Florence Kelley (1859-1932) chaired the subcommittee in charge of the project. With the help of former member of Congress Jeannette Rankin (1880-1973), who as NCL field secretary lobbied on Capitol Hill for the bill, Kelley mobilized suffrage networks in every state to persuade state legislators to appropriate the matching funds the Sheppard-Towner bill required.

Opposition was strong. Legislators, shaken by the recent Russian Revolution of 1917, reaffirmed the American tradition of limited government by opposing the idea of state bureaucracies "interfering" in family life. The American Medical Association made a similar protest, calling Sheppard-Towner "socialistic." Eventually, 44 states accepted Sheppard-Towner, but many did so only reluctantly. Congress cut funds for the program by the end of the decade, but many of its child welfare provisions later resurfaced in Title V of the 1935 Social Security Act. Moreover, some states continued to fund health education programs.

During the 1920s, women's organizations lobbied at state levels for children's codes concerning guardianship, age of consent, juvenile delinquency, care of the disabled, child support and school attendance. A National Child Labor Committee, formed in 1904, successfully lobbied for a federal law against child labor in 1916. However, the U.S. Supreme Court declared the law, and a subsequent law passed in 1919, unconstitutional on the ground that they interfered with the right of labor to contract freely.

Reformers then put their hopes in a federal child labor amendment to the Constitution, which Congress passed in 1924. Again, Florence Kelley took charge of the ratification effort. Despite endorsement from both major political parties, arguments that the amendment encroached on labor-management relations, undermined family control over children, infringed on states' rights and smacked of "state socialism" persuaded state legislatures to reject it. Eliminating the child labor blight in the United States would have to wait for the Fair Labor Standards Act (1938) of the New Deal era.

The effect of industrial poisons on workers also concerned social reformers. Alice Hamilton (1869-1970), the physician in charge of the Hull House health clinic, had met many workers suffering from radium, lead and phosphorus poisoning. In the early 1910s, with government support, she studied industrial poisons and lobbied for laws requiring safety measures and medical examinations. In the 1920s, when Hamilton was a faculty member at Harvard University, she prompted the U.S. Surgeon General to call national conferences on lead (1925) and radium (1928) poisoning. During the Depression, while acting as a consultant to the Labor Department, Hamilton demonstrated the toxic nature of the viscose rayon industry. Her work prompted the passage of compensation laws for occupational diseases and established the field of industrial medicine.

During the Depression, as many female social workers moved from private to public agencies, welfare concepts based on decades of experience in settlement houses and charitable associations moved to the government level. Innovations of settlement houses and female-headed private charities, as well as the provisions of Sheppard-Towner, formed the heart of welfare ideas, including aid to dependent children, old age, unemployment and health insurance, and public health programs.

As Franklin Roosevelt's political star rose, Eleanor Roosevelt used her own rising influence to realize a women's reform agenda. Volunteer work in settlements and for the National Consumers' League had formed Roosevelt's early social vision. During the 1920s, she became an active member of nonpartisan groups, such as the League of Women Voters, the Women's Trade Union League (WTUL), and the Women's City Club of New York, and was a mainstay of the partisan group, the Women's Division of the New York Democratic State party.

After Franklin became president in 1933, Eleanor used her regular press conferences, syndicated daily newspaper columns and countless speeches to call attention to the needs of the unemployed. She was especially concerned that relief programs assist needy women as well as men. She participated actively in planning the White House Conference on the Emergency Needs of Women in November 1933 and later worked closely with women leaders and bureaucrats in implementing the conference's ideas and projects.

Unemployment and old age insurance already were in place in many industrial countries. Progressive Era reformers had promoted these ideas as appropriate for Americans, only to be rebuffed by legislators who associated such reforms with "state socialism" and "big government." Only the deep misery of the Depression brought these legislators around.

Frances Perkins (1880-1965), whose career exemplifies how women's activism prepared them for roles in public policy, helped bring about this change. A graduate of Mount Holyoke College, Perkins taught and did volunteer settlement work before becoming secretary of the New York Consumers' League in 1910. On March 25, 1911, she witnessed the horrible Triangle Shirtwaist Factory fire, which killed 146 workers, mostly young immigrant women. She never forgot the experience.

As chair of the Committee of Safety of the City of New York, established after the fire to work for safe factory conditions, Perkins helped gather information for the New York State Factory Investigating Commission. When one of the commission's chairs, legislator Alfred E. Smith, became governor in 1919, he appointed Perkins a State Industrial Commissioner. Franklin Roosevelt later appointed Perkins Secretary of Labor. Thus she became the first female to hold a U.S. cabinet post.

In June 1934, in response to the growing misery of the Depression, President Roosevelt created a cabinet-level committee to devise a social security system. He appointed women social reformers such as Grace Abbott and Helen Hall to the committee and asked Perkins to chair it, saying, "You care about this thing, therefore I know you will put your back to it more than anybody else, and you will drive it through." Perkins became the Social Security bill's chief national advocate.

Certain aspects of the bill disappointed her. For example, she had wanted it to include health insurance, but protests from the medical profession killed the proposal. She opposed funding old age insurance through employee contributions, but since Roosevelt favored the idea, it went through. In August 1935, a Social Security bill including a federal-state system of unemployment insurance, direct relief programs and public health services such as those pioneered under Sheppard-Towner, passed Congress by a wide margin. Perkins was present when Roosevelt signed the legislation into law.

Mothers' Pensions, or payments to mothers (especially widows) without means to care for their children, was now called Aid to Dependent Children (in 1962 the name of the program was changed to Aid to Families with Dependent Children, or AFDC). The program had emerged from a Children's Bureau report written by Katharine Lenroot, Martha M. Eliot and former bureau chief Grace Abbott. Local advocates now needed to make sure the program was implemented.

Florence Fifer Bohrer was one such advocate. A former Republican state senator in Illinois (1925-33), daughter of a former governor, and League of Women Voters leader, Bohrer was instrumental in getting Illinois to make the required bureaucratic changes in all 102 counties of the state. The task was both complicated and difficult. County judges who had administered the pensions did not want to give up control. As with Sheppard-Towner, legislators resisted appropriating state monies to match federal funds. Working as a volunteer, Bohrer mastered all of the details and personally supervised the transition to the new system.

"I saw a thing to do and I did it."
—Florence Fifer Bohrer

African American Women Working Through Grassroots Institutions

Before woman suffrage, African American women had built a strong community tradition among urban blacks, setting up mutual aid societies, self-improvement clubs, temperance societies, churches, schools and orphanages. In the 1890s, educators Anna Julia Cooper (1858-1964), Mary Church Terrell (1863-1954), Mary Murray Washington (1865-1925) and journalist Ida B. Wells (1862-1931) founded women's clubs that helped African American families migrating to northern cities. In the early 1900s, social workers and women's church groups founded settlement houses to serve black neighborhoods. Mary McLeod Bethune (1875-1955), Charlotte Hawkins Brown (1883-1961), Jane Edna Harris Hunter (1882-1959) and Nannie H. Burroughs (1879-1961)—all daughters of former slaves or sharecroppers—led educational and welfare movements to aid black youth.

"Keep on going, keep on insisting, keep on fighting injustice."
—Mary Church Terrell

Working through church committees, women organized fundraisers to assist African Americans in economic trouble. Outside the churches, women school teachers instilled racial pride in children and achieved reforms such as equal pay for black teachers and improved educational conditions. Some efforts crossed racial lines. In 1920, pressure from African American women in the YWCA and white women in the Southern Methodist Women's Missionary Council forced the Council for Interracial Cooperation (CIC) to found a Women's Committee. This group focused on welfare activities and racial harmony. Meanwhile, the YWCA supported the founding of separate "colored" branches of the organization to develop character-building programs for African American girls.

Working in both informal and formal ways, Mary McLeod Bethune helped create a national commitment to better lives for African Americans. Born in South Carolina, Bethune originally trained for missionary work in Africa but instead became a teacher, a profession common among educated women. In 1904 she founded a small school for girls in Daytona Beach, Florida. By the end of the 1920s, it had evolved into the coeducational Bethune-Cookman College, with Mary Bethune as president.

Bethune participated actively in the National Association for the Advancement of Colored People (NAACP), founded in 1909 to work for civil rights, and in the National Urban League, formed in 1911 to improve job opportunities and housing for migrating blacks. A longtime leader in the National Association of Colored Women's Clubs, in 1935 she founded the National Council of Negro Women, which coordinated the work of 30 black women's groups.

During the New Deal, the National Youth Administration of the Works Progress Administration appointed Bethune a consultant to its advisory council. From this post, she eventually directed government affairs concerning African Americans, intervening when a government appointment of a black official got bogged down or when the concerns and needs of black communities were ignored in the development of social policies. In 1936, Bethune organized a Federal Council on Negro Affairs, an informal group of 27 men and three women that came to be known as the "Black Cabinet." This council met weekly at Bethune's home to hammer out priorities.

Reforming Welfare Programs

Efforts to expand the Social Security system dominated welfare reformers' concerns after the New Deal. Workers' dependents received benefits in 1939. The National Council of Negro Women, under Bethune's leadership until 1949, successfully agitated to extend Social Security benefits to domestic and agricultural workers in the 1950s.

The Social Security system assumed that all women were, or should be, dependent on a male breadwinner. Married women who worked, and the dependents and survivors of working women, did not receive full benefits. Long before the revival of the woman's movement, the National Federation of Business and Professional Women's Clubs lobbied against such inequities. During the 1970s, the Women's Equity Action League and other groups successfully pressed a case to the Supreme Court outlawing sex discrimination in the Old Age Insurance program, but other practices remained difficult to change. Despite pressure from women and senior citizens to end

Mary McLeod Bethune Speaking at Bethune-Cookman College, Daytona Beach, Florida with Eleanor Roosevelt in the Background, 1940s.

"If I touch you with one finger, you would hardly feel it. If I tapped you with two or three together, you would know you had been touched. But if I should strike with a closed fist, you would certainly know you had been hit. And that is how we must strike at our problems."

— Mary McLeod Bethune

Social Security inequities between working and nonworking women, the system still presumes women's economic dependence on men.

Challenges to government control over the private lives of women on welfare were more successful. To receive Aid to Families with Dependent Children (AFDC), women had to conform to "suitable homes" or "fit parent" provisions, which officials enforced with midnight raids of welfare homes to see if a male was present. In 1963, the protests of Los Angeles women against the raids led Johnnie Tillmon, a welfare mother, to form the Aid to Needy Children Mothers' Organization to help AFDC mothers win their rights within the welfare system. Tillmon later became a leader in the National Welfare Rights Organization, which opposed inequities in the welfare system.

Child care issues formed an important part of women's welfare concerns after World War II. During the war, a Women's Bureau survey showed that 16 percent of mothers working in war industries had no child-care arrangements. After the war, eight million mothers of young children were working outside the home. A Children's Bureau report of 1958 showed that 400,000 children lacked adequate care. In November 1960, after a National Conference on Day Care for Children, presidential candidate John F. Kennedy promised Elinor Guggenheimer, head of the National Committee on Day Care, that he would support federal funding for day care. In 1962, however, the government authorized day care funds only for children on public assistance.

Child care and preschool education have remained central to women's welfare activism. Women developed the local Head Start programs that emerged from President Lyndon Johnson's War on Poverty of the mid-1960s. Polly Greenberg, founder of the Child Development Group of Mississippi (CDGM), received Head Start funds when her state refused to apply for them. Attorney Marian Wright Edelman became an influential board member of CDGM, helping to save the program when criticism about the group's presumed misuse of funds resulted in their temporary loss. Building on her experience in women's grassroots activism for social welfare reform, Edelman later founded and directed the Children's Defense Fund, which works to correct the gap between federal programs and their implementation.

CHAPTER THREE
Rights For Women

Woman suffrage did not eliminate legal discriminations against women. Some states still gave husbands control over the earnings of their wives and minor children, or allowed husbands to determine wives' legal residence. Others limited a woman's inheritance to one-third of her husband's property, if he died without a will, but granted widowers complete control over a deceased wife's property. More than half the states continued to bar women from juries and certain public offices. Federal laws directed that a husband's citizenship determine that of his wife and restricted the circulation of birth control information.

Equal Rights Versus Equal Opportunities

Although politically active women agreed that women should have more legal and economic rights, they did not always agree on how best to proceed. Suffragist Alice Paul (1885-1977) suggested the most controversial course, arguing for a new constitutional amendment at the federal level. Her "Equal Rights Amendment" (ERA), first proposed in fall 1920, would make men and women absolutely equal before the law.

The idea of an ERA was so threatening that it split the ranks of the woman's movement. What did "equality" mean? What were its implications for women? Would they be treated exactly the "same" as men? Weren't women so different—physically, psychologically and in terms of their social roles—that treating them like men might harm rather than help them?

Many women believed that it might, although they approved of equal "opportunities" for women and wanted to remove laws that discriminated against women, especially in their family lives. Adopting the slogan "specific bills for specific ills," these women campaigned against a "blanket" equality law. They were especially concerned about the impact of such a law on the legislation that had been passed since the early 1900s to protect women in the workplace and that emphasized women's "difference" from men.

Social and industrial reformers had worked for protective laws ever since the late nineteenth century. Their original hope was to protect all workers from bad conditions. But the courts had ruled that protective laws represented an illegal interference by the state in a free marketplace. To change attitudes on this question, reformers produced research showing the effects of bad working conditions on women. Beginning with the 1908 U.S. Supreme Court decision in *Muller* v. *Oregon,* they won special protections for women, including shorter hours, longer rest periods and bans on night work.

These laws had some negative effects. They "protected" some women right out of their jobs, often the best paid jobs they could get. The laws also perpetuated stereotypes about women's "weakness" that carried over into the nonindustrial workplace. On these grounds, the National Woman's Party (NWP), under Alice Paul's leadership, opposed protectionism. Made up primarily of professional and business women, the NWP contested any law that put women in an inferior economic position. The League of Women Voters (LWV), the Women's Trade Union League (WTUL) and other social reform organizations wanted to preserve protective laws and even expand them (see Chapter 5, Labor and the Economy). They acknowledged that protections caused problems but believed that working-class women would be worse off without them.

After a concerted campaign, in 1923 the NWP succeeded in winning the first congressional hearings on the ERA. With each side in the debate claiming to represent the best interests of all women, and also testifying vigorously against the opposing view, Congress took no action. The amendment lay dormant for many years, until it was revived after World War II and again during the early 1970s.

Common Goals

Despite their divisions after suffrage, organized women worked together on some issues, including independent citizenship rights for women. A 1907 law requiring women to take on the citizenship of their husbands had led to many problems, including the barring of American women in some states from certain professions, such as the law, or from holding a civil service post because they had become "aliens" through marriage.

The Association of Women Lawyers, led by Ellen Spencer Mussey, had worked to abolish the 1907 law before suffrage but made little progress. After suffrage, the League of Women Voters took up the project, winning endorsement from the major political parties. Ohio Representative John L. Cable, in consultation with Maud Wood Park, LWV president, and the Women's Joint Congressional Committee, proposed a reform bill. The Cable Act, or Married Women's Independent Citizenship Act, passed Congress on September 22, 1922. In 1931, thanks to active lobbying by Suma Sugi (representing the Japanese American Citizens League) and other women's groups, the Cable Act was amended to eliminate citizenship inequities based on race.

Both sides in the ERA debate also cooperated on winning women's right to jury service. Women had served as jurors briefly in Wyoming Territory in 1871, but in 1879 the U.S. Supreme Court, in *Strauder* v. *West Virginia*, permitted a state to confine jury duty to males. Before the ratification of the Nineteenth Amendment in 1920, 16 states already had given the franchise to women, but only five of these (Idaho, Kansas, Michigan, Nevada and Utah) permitted women to serve on juries. After suffrage, only 21 states allowed jury service for women.

The National Woman's Party, the League of Women Voters, and members of women's civic and professional clubs across the nation worked for years to remove the gender-specific language of jury provisions while allowing exemptions from service to anyone, female or male, with dependents at home. By 1927, Ohio, the Territory of Alaska, the District of Columbia and Rhode Island had legalized women jurors. New York's campaign took until 1937, Connecticut's almost as long. Tennessee kept women off juries until 1951, South Carolina until 1967. Most women's service remained optional until the U.S. Supreme Court case in *Taylor* v. *Louisiana* (1976), which required all juries to reflect a "fair cross section of the community."

Many women favored another women's issue of the time, the legalization of access to information about birth control. In 1873, as part of a moral purity campaign, reformer Anthony Comstock persuaded Congress to pass a bill declaring contraceptive information obscene and thus banned from the U.S. mails. Wealthy women could still gain access to information from private doctors, but many women continued to suffer grave economic and physical tolls from multiple, unplanned pregnancies.

Women who worked for birth control also promoted the idea that women, like men, should be able to enjoy sexual expression separate from reproduction. One was anarchist Emma Goldman (1869-1940). A trained nurse and midwife, Goldman agitated in her speeches and writings for the lifting of all sanctions against contraceptive information. Goldman and another nurse, Margaret Sanger (1879-1966), suffered fines and arrests for distributing such information.

Sanger went on to make access to birth control, a term she coined, her life's work. She publicized information in her journal *The Woman Rebel* (1914), and with her sister Edith Byrne founded the first birth-control advice center (1916). To win wider support, she increasingly and successfully allied herself with the medical community. This tactic brought success. In 1921, Sanger organized the American Birth Control League, and in 1923 founded the Birth Control Clinical Research Bureau in New York City. By this time, her cause had lost much of its radical character. Even though major religious groups still opposed birth control, and states still insisted on restricting access to birth control information, mainstream women's groups began to support the cause.

In 1936, Sanger's Committee on Federal Legislation for Birth Control won the Supreme Court case, *United States* v. *One Package*, a victory that ended the obscenity classification of birth-control information. Birth-control advocates across the country rushed to found clinics modeled on Sanger's Research Bureau. By 1938, more than 300 had been established. Thereafter, the movement increasingly emphasized family stability over women's individual free choice. In 1942, reflecting this shift, the movement's chief organization was renamed the Planned Parenthood Federation.

During the 1940s, the economic disadvantages of laws that specifically protected women in the workplace became increasingly obvious and ironic. For example, bans on night work for women sometimes prevented women from waiting tables or tending bar at night, when tips were highest, but not charwomen from cleaning offices at night. And since the Fair Labor Standards Act, passed in 1938 during the Depression, established the principle that government could regulate conditions for all workers, preserving special protections for women now seemed less critical. World War II demonstrated that women could do men's work without physical harm. In fact, women served with distinction during the war, both on the production line and in the military, sometimes under combat conditions.

Support for an ERA began to grow among organizations that previously had opposed it, such as the General Federation of Women's Clubs and the National Education Association. Opposition continued, however, from a coalition called the

Women march in Washington, DC to Support the Equal Rights Amendment, August 26, 1977.

National Committee on the Status of Women. This group worked to remove women's legal disabilities and prohibit sex discrimination, but insisted on exceptions based on physical, biological and social differences between men and women.

Unable to agree on an ERA, during the 1940s and 1950s women activists focused instead on equal pay. Although their efforts failed to win congressional action, some dozen states passed equal pay legislation. Other state gains included laws that gave women access to the same educational and professional opportunities open to men and allowed them to work without their husbands' permission. Women's organizations such as the YWCA began to take stronger stands, arguing for equity for women in Social Security legislation, for example. League of Women Voters leaders, such as South Carolina's Barbara Moxon, protested the disfranchisement of armed service wives. Although their husbands could vote by absentee ballot, military wives could not.

Consciousness Raising

During the 1950s, at the height of the postwar emphasis on women's domesticity that author Betty Friedan would label the "feminine mystique," women's organizations flourished, especially at community levels. In national partisan politics, however, women's influence declined. In 1952, the national Democratic party abolished its Women's Division, a source of strength, funding and solidarity for party women since the 1920s. India Edwards, its director, became a vice-chair of the party but no longer had her own staff. Republican women were similarly marginalized.

Women's political consciousness was rising, however. In 1955, lesbians Del Martin and Phyllis Lyon founded the Daughters of Bilitis (DOB), one of the groups, along with the Mattachine Society, that served as a foundation of the later gay and lesbian rights movement. Signs of discontent appeared among women in clerical, service and factory work, who were earning, on average, 60 percent of what men earned. Although educational opportunities for women were expanding, few women advanced up professional ladders, and most women remained economically dependent on their husbands.

In 1960, Esther Peterson became Assistant Secretary of Labor and Director of the Women's Bureau, the highest-ranking woman in President Kennedy's administration. An active unionist, she opposed an ERA but agreed that the government should investigate the growing concerns about women's status in the family, economy, politics and law. Peterson persuaded Kennedy to appoint a presidential Commission on the Status of Women. With Eleanor Roosevelt as its titular head (she died before the final report was issued), Peterson directed the commission's work. She drew its membership from labor unions, women's organizations and government agencies. Its 1963 final report compromised on an ERA, saying that an amendment was not needed "now." More importantly, the report detailed discrimination against women in employment and before the law, and outlined the need for more social services for women, especially child care.

The creation of commissions on the status of women in all 50 states created new grassroots networks to work for change. President Kennedy ordered the civil service to use only merit as a criterion for career positions. A federal Equal Pay Act, first proposed in 1945 and passed finally in 1963, forbade differential pay rates for men and women doing the same work. In the first ten years of its enforcement, 171,000 employees won $84 million in back pay. Despite the act's many shortcomings, these results marked a significant triumph.

Visibility and Change

Betty Friedan's book, *The Feminine Mystique* (1963), fell upon ground already prepared. Agitation for civil rights helped cement the path toward the resurgence of feminism. In 1964, during the congressional debate on the Civil Rights Act, Representative Howard W. Smith of Virginia added the word "sex," along with race, color, religion and national origin, to the conditions of discrimination that the act would outlaw. A supporter of racial segregation, he hoped that the addition would kill the bill.

Some members of Congress laughed at the idea of "sex" as a basis for prohibiting discrimination, but Representative Martha Griffiths, Senator Margaret Chase Smith and other women's rights activists succeeded in getting the act passed with the word "sex" in place in 1964. The act's Title VII became the strongest legal statement against discrimination on the basis of sex ever enacted by the federal government.

An Equal Employment Opportunity Commission (EEOC) was established to enforce the Civil Rights Act. When the commission refused to endorse an end to separate employment advertisements for men and women and failed to pursue other sex discrimination complaints with sufficient vigor, protests mounted. Delegates to the third National Conference of State Commissions on the Status of Women met with Betty Friedan and organized the National Organization for Women (NOW) in 1966. With this step, a new women's movement announced its birth.

A younger stream of women entered the movement through civil rights work. During the Freedom Summers of 1964 and 1965 (see Chapter 4, Women in the Civil Rights Movement), hundreds of volunteers, many of them women, went south to help register African Americans to vote. When a few of the women volunteers drew attention to ways in which they felt their work was unappreciated, they met ridicule. Some of these women withdrew, forming small discussion groups of like-minded women to seek strength through a collective sharing of experiences and feelings. These consciousness-raising or "CR" groups, which reflected traditional female techniques for grass-roots community work, spread like wildfire.

Other more dramatic techniques of consciousness raising began to attract media attention. Some activists engaged in guerrilla theater, or confrontational public demonstrations of their views. At the 1968 Miss America contest, protesters trashed bras, girdles and high heels, all items representing the exploitation of women as sexual objects. The event gave birth to the term "bra burner," a misnomer later applied indiscriminately to feminists. Other groups picketed the *New York Times* to protest its sex-typed job advertisements and disrupted congressional hearings to demand the legalization of abortion.

In the early 1970s, sexual discrimination suits multiplied. NOW's "Women's Strike for Equality" on August 26, 1970, the 50th anniversary of woman suffrage, attracted huge nationwide support. Despite the longstanding social stigma associated with the term "feminist," thousands of women across the nation now identified with the women's movement. Under widespread pressure from their employees and clients, leaders of major publications, businesses and educational institutions slowly began to enact changes in hiring and promotion practices.

By 1972, all of the major women's organizations—the League of Women Voters, the American Association of University Women, the Business and Professional Women's Clubs, the National Council of Negro Women and the Young Women's Christian Association—now supported an ERA. On March 22, 1972, some 50 years after its first introduction, Congress finally voted to approve the Equal Rights Amendment. Twenty-two states rushed to ratify. Then the process stalled, as an anti-feminist backlash swelled.

Led by Phyllis Schlafly, ERA opponents raised enough fears about its potential for harm to convince the remaining state legislatures to withhold approval. Would an ERA require women to be drafted and sent into combat? Would federal payments for abortion be put on the same level as payments for all medical treatments? Would divorced mothers be forced to support their children and lose access to alimony? Would public toilets, prisons and hospital facilities be integrated?

In all probability, an Equal Rights Amendment would have had none of these effects, but no one knew for sure. With feminists exaggerating the amendment's potential benefits and anti-feminists its potential for harm, some states that had ratified the amendment voted to rescind approval. Despite a two-year extension of the ratification deadline, the ERA fell three states short of the 38 needed to ratify.

Despite the defeat of the ERA, women's movement activists cheered other victories during the 1970s. Title IX of the 1972

Higher Education Act prohibited discrimination on the basis of sex in any program financed by federal funds. This provision paved the way for better funding for women's athletic programs. Other victories included tax breaks to working parents for child care costs and the expansion of the enforcement capability of the Equal Employment Opportunity Commission.

New activist organizations were born. In 1971, Betty Friedan, Bella Abzug and Shirley Chisholm helped found the National Women's Political Caucus (NWPC), a nonpartisan organization to promote women's political participation. The following year, women's participation in the national conventions of the major political parties tripled. Chisholm launched a campaign for the presidency, the first African American woman to do so, and Frances "Sissy" Farenthold received 420 votes when her name was offered for the Democratic party nomination for vice-president. Both major party platforms adopted planks promoted by women, including support for an ERA, antidiscrimination laws, tax and educational equity, and the extension of the Equal Pay Act.

Some nonlegislative changes concerning women took on great importance in the 1970s. The 7-2 ruling in the 1973 Supreme Court case of *Roe* v. *Wade* affirmed women's right to privacy in abortion decisions. Like the ERA, *Roe* led to a backlash that still can be felt in the 1990s. In 1976, the National Right to Life Committee and other groups convinced Congress to prohibit federal funding for abortions for poor women.

Institutional changes resulting from the women's movement included major shifts in social attitudes toward rape, the battering of women and the sexual rights of husbands. Rape crisis centers, battered women's shelters, women's health collectives, feminist journals and bookstores, and lesbian collectives appeared, primarily in urban centers but across the entire country.

As a result of the work of organized women for change, women's status will always be a topic of debate in this country. Not everyone will agree on what it should be. But it will never again be what it was before women won the vote.

CHAPTER FOUR

WOMEN IN THE CIVIL RIGHTS MOVEMENT

Women have played vital roles in the struggle of American minority groups for their civil rights. In most civil rights movements, men led the marches and demonstrations, held executive positions in movement organizations and captured the headlines. But women did much of the organizational work that sustained the movements from day to day, and some held leadership posts that determined the direction movements took.

Exposing Racism and Discrimination

After Reconstruction, African Americans faced increased racial discrimination. In both South and North, literacy tests, poll taxes and property requirements restricted African Americans' voting rights. They received only the lowest-paid work in the South's new industries and, as sharecroppers, became entrapped in permanent cycles of debt. Jim Crow laws, legitimized by Supreme Court rulings such as *Plessy* v. *Ferguson* (1896), kept the races separated in schools and public places.

Lynchings and race riots multiplied around the turn of the century. An especially violent riot in Springfield, Illinois in 1908 led to a protest meeting of African Americans, including scholar W. E. B. Du Bois, held in Niagara Falls, Canada. The following year, these leaders joined concerned whites, such as Mary White Ovington, a civil rights reformer who had lived in African American neighborhoods, to form the National Association for the Advancement of Colored People (NAACP).

By 1914, the NAACP had 6,000 members and 50 branches, some founded by women, such as Nettie Asberry of Tacoma, Washington. Although male lawyers dominated its hierarchy, women exercised leadership by working to increase economic security in the African American community. Building on the tradition of community service they had established in the 1800s, women founded social settlements, homes for single mothers and numerous educational institutions.

Some women worked directly as journalists and agitators for civil rights. In 1892, Ida B. Wells (later, Wells-Barnett), an African American newspaper editor from Memphis, Tennessee, revealed the economic motives behind the lynching of three black grocery store owners. In retaliation, her office was destroyed and her life threatened. She devoted the rest of her career to national and international campaigns against lynching. Wells-Barnett exposed as sham the lynch mob's excuse of protecting white women from black male rapists and discussed openly white male abuse of black women. After moving to Illinois, she also founded African American suffrage clubs and integrated the state's suffrage movement.

Jessie Daniel Ames, a white social reformer and former suffragist in Texas, fought racial discrimination through her association with the Council for Interracial Cooperation. In 1930, she founded the Association of Southern Women for the Prevention of Lynching (ASWPL). Through networks of black and white women's organizations, the ASWPL launched educational campaigns to expose the myths surrounding lynching, investigated lynchings that occurred and pressured officials to prosecute.

In the early years following suffrage, ideals of racial cooperation and equality were not widely accepted. Few of the organizations dominated by white women made racial equality a priority. In her pursuit of equal rights for women, Alice Paul defined African American women's push for voting rights as a "race," not a "woman's," issue. Organizations such as the League of Women Voters focused on welfare and political reforms. When, in the 1930s, Mary McLeod Bethune's National Council of Negro Women started an interracial coalition of women's organizations called the Co-ordinating Committee for Building Better Race Relations, only the YWCA, the National Women's Trade Union League and women's religious organizations responded favorably.

There were individual exceptions. Eleanor Roosevelt, for example, took public stands on racial equality, supporting civil rights organizations such as the Southern Conference for Human Welfare. At its 1938 Birmingham, Alabama meeting, as a protest against Jim Crow laws, Roosevelt sat by herself in the aisle between the white and colored sections of the hall. The following year, she resigned publicly from the Daughters of the American Revolution after it refused to rent its hall to African American singer Marian Anderson. She used her syndicated column, *My Day,* as a forum to promote ideas of racial harmony and convinced her husband to take constructive action toward ending economic discrimination against African Americans.

During the 1930s and 1940s, women of other ethnic groups led civil rights campaigns. In 1939, labor organizer Luisa Moreno (1906-1993) was a principal organizer for "El Congreso De Pueblos Que Hablan Española" ("Spanish-speaking Peoples' Congress"), the first national civil rights assembly

> *"I would not have expected that I, who am barely out of savagery, would have to remind gentlemen with five thousand years of recorded civilization behind them of our Bill of Rights."*
> —Elizabeth Wanamaker Peratrovich

of Latinos. The congress met in April and adopted a comprehensive platform demanding political representation, immigrant rights, bilingual education, and an end to segregation in public facilities, housing, education and employment.

Native American women also were active. Recognized as U.S. citizens after 1924, Native Americans nonetheless experienced rampant discrimination and loss of rights over their lands. Through assimilation, Native American cultures were fast disappearing. As president of the General Federation of Women's Clubs, musician Roberta Campbell Lawson, or MingOMeNow (1878-1940), a Delaware from Oklahoma, gave monthly radio broadcasts in the interests of preserving Native American culture. At her death, her collection of early American artifacts and research library went to the Philbrook Museum of Oklahoma. Gertrude Simmons Bonnin, or Zitkala-sa (1875-1938), a Sioux activist and president of the National Council of American Indians, believed in assimilation but fought hard to preserve the property rights of Oklahoma's Five Civilized Tribes and to protect the welfare of Native American children.

The Alaska Native Brotherhood (ANB) and Sisterhood (ANS), founded in 1912 and 1915, led campaigns for Native American civil rights in Alaska Territory. In 1929 they organized a boycott of movie theaters that ended segregated seating. In the 1940s, however, their bills to prohibit other discriminatory practices met defeat. As ANS Grand Camp President in 1945, Elizabeth Wanamaker Peratrovich (1911-1958), a Tlingit, spearheaded an antidiscrimination bill. Although it passed the territorial House easily, the Senate balked. Some members expressed racist views, including Senator Allen Shattuck, who asked, "Who are these people, barely out of savagery, who want to associate with us whites with 5,000 years of recorded civilization behind us?"

When observers had a chance to comment, Peratrovich rose to speak. "I would not have expected," she said, "that I, who am barely out of savagery, would have to remind gentlemen with five thousand years of recorded civilization behind them of our Bill of Rights." An elegant, well spoken woman, she told of the discrimination she and her family had experienced. The Senate passed the bill 11 to 5. Territorial governor Ernest Gruening, himself a champion of civil rights, later attributed the bill's passage to Peratrovich's skillful and persistent advocacy.

During World War II, the forced relocation into inland internment camps of more than a hundred thousand west coast American citizens of Japanese origin provoked Japanese American women into renewed activism. Miné Okubo (b. 1912), an artist, kept an illustrated record of everything she observed in the federal "assembly center" to which she had been removed. Years later, working through the National Coalition for Redress and Reparations (NCRR), Tsuyako "Sox" Kitashima (b. 1918) testified in Washington, lobbied Congress and mailed more than 25,000 letters to win passage of a bill granting internees reparations and a national apology. The bill was finally signed by President Reagan in 1988.

Grassroots Tactics Shape the Movement

Spurred by the U.S. entry into World War II, the campaign for African American civil rights heightened in the early 1940s. African American leaders succeeded in convincing the Roosevelt administration that a war against racism abroad required one at home. President Roosevelt eventually banned discrimination in defense industries and job-training programs.

Customary discrimination elsewhere in society was harder to eradicate. The Congress of Racial Equality (CORE), founded in spring 1942, began to experiment with sit-ins at segregated restaurants. Individual protest actions against segregation on public transportation increased. In 1940, two African American women, Pauli Murray (1910-1985), a political activist and writer, and her friend, Adelene McBean, traveled to Durham, North Carolina on a Greyhound bus. During a stop in Petersburg, Virginia, the women challenged the driver's demand that they move further back. They were arrested.

The NAACP wanted to use their arrest to test the legality of segregation on interstate transport but had to drop the idea when the judge ruled that the women had "created a disturbance." In 1944, similar cases arose. The NAACP brought to the Supreme Court the case of Irene Morgan, arrested at Saluda, Virginia for refusing to give up her bus seat to a white man. In *Morgan v. Virginia*, the Court declared Virginia's racially biased seating rules invalid.

In the early 1940s, Ruth Powell, a Howard University student, campaigned alone against segregated restaurants in Washington, DC. Inspired by Mohandas K. Gandhi's civil disobedience against British rule in India and CORE's nonviolent actions in the U.S., Powell sat quietly when refused service, sometimes for hours, staring at waiters or asking them to name the law they were enforcing. In January 1943, Powell, Marianne Musgrave and Juanita Morrow ordered hot chocolates at a downtown Washington store. When the waitress refused to serve them, they called for the manager and refused to leave. The waitress eventually served the three women but then overcharged them. After insisting on paying only the correct amount, they were arrested.

Protest meetings over the hot chocolate incident led to more sit-ins. In April 1943, authorized by the Howard University NAACP, Powell organized small groups of carefully prepared students, who entered the "Little Palace," a cafeteria in the heart of a mostly African American community. When refused service, the groups took empty trays to tables. Soon they filled the place. Picketers pointed out the irony of African Americans serving the war effort while being denied equality at home. After two days, the owner gave in and served the students.

Twelve of the original 19 Howard student protesters were women. Ruth Powell later became chief of service at the Bronx Psychiatric Center in New York City; Juanita Morrow became an active leader of CORE sit-ins; and the youngest member of the group, Patricia Roberts (later, Harris), was Secretary of the Department of Housing and Urban Development (HUD) and then of Health and Human Services (HHS) under President Carter. Other participants who became lawyers went on to defend civil rights demonstrators in the 1960s.

The Montgomery Women's Political Council (WPC), founded by Alabama State College English professor Mary Fair Burks, played a pivotal role in the civil rights movement of the 1950s. In 1946, police arrested and beat Burks for allegedly using profanity in addressing a white pedestrian. Although the charges were dropped, the experience prompted Burks to organize her professional women friends to fight racism.

WPC members registered voters and protested abuses on city buses and in segregated parks. They waged educational campaigns, teaching students about democracy and training adults to pass literacy tests. When 15-year-old Claudette Colvin was arrested in March 1955 for refusing to give up her bus seat, the WPC and other local civil rights groups discussed a bus boycott. They abandoned the idea when the charge against the young woman, who turned out to be pregnant, was changed to resisting arrest. On December 1, 1955, however, Montgomery resident Rosa Parks (b. 1913), a department store seamstress, was arrested for refusing to give up her seat to a white man. In response, WPC leaders, including president Jo Ann Gibson Robinson and members Uretta Adair and Irene West, launched the bus boycott plan that led ultimately to the Supreme Court decision outlawing segregation on city buses.

Parks represents the organized grassroots activism of southern African American women. Secretary of the Montgomery NAACP and active in the St. Paul AME Church, a center of resistance to discrimination, Parks long had complained of the treatment of African Americans on buses. Virginia Durr, a white anti-poll tax crusader for whom Parks had occasionally worked, had urged her to accept a scholarship to the Highlander Folk School in Monteagle, Tennessee. This famous biracial school for labor organizers had trained Parks and many others in the techniques of peaceful civil disobedience.

At Highlander, Parks met Septima Poinsette Clark (1898-1987), a former teacher from South Carolina. Clark's grassroots racial work began in 1935 with education programs for black soldiers and a successful campaign to equalize the pay of African American teachers. She then became active in the YWCA, attended Highlander Folk School workshops and served as membership chair for the Charleston NAACP. In 1956, the government of South Carolina stipulated that no public employee, including teachers, could affiliate with a civil rights organization. When Clark refused to give up her work, she lost her job and retirement benefits. With support from Highlander, she developed "citizenship schools" for literacy training and democratic empowerment. In 1961, she became director of education and teaching for the Southern Christian Leadership Conference (SCLC), the organization that built on the momentum of the Montgomery boycott.

Modjeska Simkins (1899-1992), a teacher, began her activism as director of Negro Work for the South Carolina Tuberculosis Association (1931-1942). In this post she raised money and developed workshops, institutes and conferences to promote health education. In 1939, she helped found the South Carolina Conference of the NAACP. A few years later, the Tuberculosis Association dismissed her, ostensibly for budgetary reasons but in fact because of her activism. After working on a successful campaign to equalize teachers' salaries, Simkins assisted the South Carolina NAACP Conference in *Elmore* v. *Rice* (1947) and *Brown* v. *Baskins* (1948), cases that sought to dismantle the state's white election primary and restore full voting rights to blacks. In 1949, with the help of NAACP lawyer Thurgood Marshall, the conference launched *Briggs* v. *Elliot*, the first Supreme Court desegregation case. To show that segregation was not confined to the South, the NAACP later combined *Briggs* with *Brown* v. *Board of Education of Topeka, Kansas,* the landmark case that outlawed segregated schools. As the state NAACP conference secretary, Simkins wrote parts of the *Briggs* brief and coordinated relief work for those who were harassed for becoming plaintiffs.

Women also served on the front lines of the civil rights movement, participating at considerable personal risk in meetings of civil rights groups and in voter registration efforts. Women organized boycotts and demonstrations. They were plaintiffs in test cases. They provided shelter and support for the volunteers who spread across the South to register voters. They swelled the ranks of the marchers, the participants at mass meetings, the jailed and the beaten. Their homes were bombed. Some died. Viola Liuzzo, a community activist from Detroit, was murdered in her car by nightriders after the Selma, Alabama march of March 21, 1965.

Ella Josephine Baker (1903-1986), born in Norfolk, Virginia and educated at Shaw University in Raleigh, North Carolina, was a prominent front-line civil rights worker. As she said, however, "you didn't see me on television, you didn't see news stories about me. The kind of role that I tried to play was to pick up pieces or put together pieces out of which I hoped organization might come. My theory is, strong people don't need strong leaders."

Baker's civil rights activism took root in Harlem. In 1930,

she joined the Young Negroes' Cooperative League, attracted to its lack of hierarchy, full inclusion of women and emphasis on grassroots community empowerment. She became its first national director in 1931. In the 1940s, she served as a field secretary and later national director of branches for the NAACP. In 1946, having developed concerns that the organization stressed fundraising, winning in court and impressing government officials over grassroots political action, she resigned her post but stayed on as a volunteer. In 1957 she helped found the Southern Christian Leadership Council, setting up its first office in Atlanta and coordinating its voter rights campaign. Eventually she came to criticize SCLC's increasing reliance on the personal charisma of African American ministers instead of on members' own leadership skills.

The modern sit-in movement began in the South in 1960. One of its centers was Nashville, Tennessee, where Fisk University student Diane Nash played a prominent role. The sit-in movement appealed to Ella Baker's belief in the power of grassroots activism. With a small grant from the SCLC, in April 1960 she called the conference of student sit-in leaders at Shaw University that led to the founding of the Student Non-Violent Coordinating Committee (SNCC). Baker infused this organization with her nonhierarchical, decentralized leadership ideas. The results were SNCC's voter registration drives, Freedom Schools (which informed African Americans of their constitutional rights) and other community projects.

In 1962, Fannie Lou Hamer (1917-1977) attended a voter registration meeting in Ruleville, Mississippi, where she worked as a sharecropper. After hearing speeches by James Forman of SNCC and James Bevel of SCLC, she joined 17 others in an attempt to register to vote. After failing the literacy test, Hamer resolved to return every month until she passed it. She was finally registered in January 1963 but in the process was fired from her job. She and her family also suffered physical harassment, including shots fired at their house. Hamer's arm was per-

"All my life I've been sick and tired. Now I'm sick and tired of being sick and tired."

—Fannie Lou Hamer

manently injured from beatings she received in jail.

As SNCC field secretary, Hamer, who was a gifted singer and speaker, inspired many recruits to join the movement. In 1964, she captured national attention as cochair of the Mississippi Freedom Democratic Party (MFDP) at the Atlanta convention of the national Democratic party. Although the Credentials Committee found Hamer's testimony moving, she failed to unseat the all-white delegation from her state. Afterwards, she refused to accept a compromise in which two MFDP members would be seated as "token" delegates-at-large. Later, with colleagues Victoria Jackson Gray and Annie Devine, Hamer challenged the legality of the Mississippi congressional delegation in Washington. Torn by dissension, the MFDP eventually fell apart, but the biracial Loyalist Democrats of Mississippi finally unseated the regular delegation at the 1968 Democratic party convention in Chicago.

There were many non-African American "troops" in the civil rights movement. Anne McCarty Braden (b. 1924), an Alabama native, was radicalized by her experiences as a journalist covering the courts. When she and her husband Carl sold their Louisville, Kentucky home to an African American family, Carl was jailed. Accused of being "communist agitators," the couple went on to become field secretaries for the Southern Conference Educational Fund, heir to the Southern Conference for Human Welfare. During the Freedom Summers of 1964 and 1965, of the hundreds of mostly white volunteers who traveled across the country to work in Mississippi and the Deep South, about half were women. Sandra ("Casey") Cason, Mary King, Jane Stembridge and Sue Thrasher were among those who worked in various phases of the movement, teaching African American history in Freedom Schools, and staffing communications systems, libraries and voter registration drives.

The modern civil rights movement evolved into a movement for black power. Kathleen Cleaver and Angela Davis are among the many women remembered for their radical, and sometimes disruptive and violent, activism for civil rights. A more dominant image of African American women's political activism of the 1970s, however, is that of Barbara Jordan, member of Congress from Texas. Her integrity, oratorical skills and commanding presence during the House Judiciary Committee hearings on the impeachment of President Nixon transcended sexual and racial stereotypes and commanded the admiration of the country.

CHAPTER FIVE

LABOR AND THE ECONOMY

Conflicts over changing working and economic conditions almost always have had political dimensions. Over the years, employers have appealed to the state to take action in times of worker protest, and national economic crises often have provoked a political response. Similarly, the views and actions of women workers, union organizers and industrial reformers have influenced the development of the nation's public policies on labor and economic issues.

Which Side Are You On?

In the nineteenth century, as the United States became industrialized, women of many ethnic backgrounds entered factory work and soon were leading protests against increasingly harsh working conditions. In the 1820s and 1830s, for example, when an economic depression led employers in the textile industry to raise the boarding costs of women workers while cutting their wages, New England women mill workers organized protests. In the 1840s, women engaged in labor violence, using sticks and stones to break down the gates of an Allegheny mill and then shutting down the looms. In the great 1860 strike among Lynn, Massachusetts shoemakers, women organized their own associations, marched and held strike meetings.

The numbers of women working outside the home rose steadily throughout the nineteenth century. In some industries, such as shoemaking and textiles, women dominated the workforce. Sometimes women workers formed trade unions or "protective associations" in their trades, but these did not last long. Some women wage-workers joined mixed-sex unions, but most male unionists did not welcome women members. Men believed that women workers drove wages down by accepting jobs at pay rates lower than men would accept, but they refused to support women's campaigns for equal pay. To many men, "woman's place was in the home," even though most women workers needed the wages they earned in order to survive.

After a brief period in the 1880s when women made up about 10 percent of the membership of the Knights of Labor, one of the nation's first labor unions, women's trade union participation declined. By 1900, only 2.2 percent of union members were women. At the time, union activity still lacked legitimacy. Employers could use force to prevent union meetings and fire union organizers and members at will. When workers struck, employers used the courts to declare the action an illegal "conspiracy" in restraint of trade. Such judgments allowed employers to use the state militia against strikers.

For women to be involved in unions at all during this period entailed risks that few could afford. Elizabeth Gurley Flynn (1890-1964) was among few women doing radical union work in the early twentieth century. Born into a family of Irish socialists, Flynn began speech-making in 1906. An eloquent and powerful speaker, she agitated for socialist groups and the Industrial Workers of the World (IWW). Flynn also participated actively in strikes and free speech demonstrations, and in 1920 she was a founding member of the American Civil Liberties Union (ACLU). In 1926, Flynn became a member of the American branch of the Communist party and remained committed to left-wing politics the rest of her life.

Middle-class social workers took a different approach to labor reform, seeking laws to protect workers from abuse and exploitation. In the 1890s Florence Kelley, then residing at Chicago's Hull House, investigated "sweated" labor conditions. Enacted largely through her efforts, an 1893 Illinois law prohibited child labor, limited working hours for women and controlled sweatshop conditions. In 1899, Kelley became general secretary of the National Consumers' League (NCL), formed to convince women to buy goods only from factories with decent working conditions. For half a century, both before and after woman suffrage, the NCL led national movements to pass protective legislation, outlaw child labor, improve conditions for retail sales clerks, develop a workers' compensation system and establish a minimum wage.

Organizing Women's Power

After the turn of the century, immigration to the United States from southern and eastern Europe swelled, bringing with it large numbers of women workers. Expansion in the ready-made clothing industry provided jobs, but working conditions were terrible. Factories were neither sanitary nor safe. Women toiled up to 14 hours a day, six days a week, more in the busy season. Pay was low, and frequently cut. There was no job security or compensation for injury.

Still generally ignored by the skilled male unionists, women garment workers began to turn elsewhere for organizational

> *"There is no reason why a working girl should be poor. Men bakers, for instance, who are organized get good wages. Girls working in such a prosperous business as the candy industry get starvation wages because they are not organized."*
>
> —Rose Schneiderman

support. The Women's Trade Union League (WTUL), founded in 1903 by college-educated, middle- to upper-class women active in social and industrial reform, proved receptive. The WTUL paid the salaries of women union organizers, provided financial, organizational and moral support to striking workers, and pressured politicians to pass labor legislation. It also brought workers into the suffrage movement. Although the WTUL's cross-class alliance did not always run smoothly, the organization was one of few in which women from different social classes worked together.

In the early 1900s, Rose Schneiderman (1882-1972), a cap maker of Polish Jewish origin, worked to organize women garment workers into unions. Although elected a union officer, she eventually became frustrated with the domination of men in union hierarchies. In 1917, she resigned her union posts and became president of the New York branch of the WTUL, with which she had been associated since 1905. In 1926, Schneiderman became president of the national WTUL, a post she held until its office closed in 1950. She was a close friend of Eleanor Roosevelt, who had joined the WTUL in the early 1920s. During the New Deal, Schneiderman was the only woman on the labor advisory board of the National Recovery Administration.

One of women's important postsuffrage victories on the labor front was the creation in 1920 of the Women's Bureau in the U.S. Department of Labor. The bureau's purpose was to collect information about women workers and advocate protective legislation for women. As states also created women's bureaus, women industrial reformers began to enter state labor departments in significant numbers.

Reformer Frances Perkins already held a powerful post in a

Frances Perkins, Secretary of Labor, and First Woman to Hold a Cabinet Appointment, Attends President Roosevelt's Signing of the Social Security Act, Washington, DC, 1935.

state labor department. As New York State's Industrial Commissioner since 1919, Perkins settled strikes in the field, reorganized the state's Factory Inspection Division, reduced the workweek from 54 to 48 hours and developed emergency relief systems for New York's jobless during the early years of the Depression. As U.S. Secretary of Labor (1933-1945), she mediated labor disputes, wrote the president's labor speeches and helped draft legislation for emergency relief, public works programs, the legalization of unions, social security, unemployment insurance and fair labor standards.

Perkins's stands on women's labor issues dissatisfied some women's rights activists. She continued to oppose an Equal Rights Amendment and she supported Section 213 of the Economy Act, which prohibited husbands and wives from holding civil service jobs at the same time. The General Federation of Women's Clubs led a coordinated effort of national women's organizations that ultimately won the repeal of Section 213.

Nonetheless, women labor activists were pleased to have "one of their own" reach cabinet level. They also made headway in other areas, such as the education of women workers for leadership. Bryn Mawr College President M. Carey Thomas and Dean Hilda Worthington Smith devised a plan for summer schools at Bryn Mawr for women workers. The school would bring together workers and college faculty for the study of history, economics, and labor organizing and negotiation.

Mary Anderson, chief of the U.S. Women's Bureau, and Rose Schneiderman helped develop the plan. With the support of Bryn Mawr's board, alumnae, faculty and students, the project began in 1921 with 82 students representing 49 trades and 25 countries of origin. The Bryn Mawr Summer School for Women Workers lasted until the late 1930s, when the college's board and alumnae decided that the school's leadership had become too radical.

The Bryn Mawr school trained women who later became union leaders. Rose Pesotta (1896-1965), who was born in the Ukraine, became a garment worker in New York in 1913. Two years later she helped Local 25 of the International Ladies' Garment Workers Union (ILGWU) set up its first education department and, in 1920, won election to the local union's executive board. After attending the Bryn Mawr Summer School in 1922, Pesotta attended Brookwood Labor College and then spent many years organizing women workers for the ILGWU. In 1934, she won election as an ILGWU vice-president, becoming the only woman on the General Executive Board of a union made up of 85 percent female workers. In 1942, frustrated with this "tokenism," Pesotta resigned from the board and returned to sewing.

Women's labor activism increased during the Depression. With the founding of the Congress of Industrial Organizations (CIO) and the organization of workers by industry, women whose labor had been classified as "unskilled" now found greater support. Still, unions were far from ready to encourage women to become leaders. In 1929-1930 and in 1934, strikes flared in southern textile plants. Despite the large presence of striking female workers, the unions rarely sent women organizers.

Throughout the Depression, many women workers marched in picket lines and participated in "sit-down" strikes for union recognition. A radical "Ladies' Auxiliary" supported a 1934 trucker's strike of Minneapolis Teamsters. Led by Clara Dunne and Marvel Scholl, the auxiliary raised money, fed thousands of people a day in the union commissary and staffed the picket lines. When the strike turned bloody, Scholl drove injured workers through back streets to escape the police and confronted City Hall with demands for an end to police interference with pickets.

During the automobile workers' sit-down strike in the winter of 1936-1937 in Flint, Michigan, wives of strikers helped ensure the strike's success. When workers associated with the United Auto Workers (UAW) occupied the Fisher Body plants

Members of the Women's Emergency Brigade with Sharpened Two-by-Fours, Ready to Defend Their Union Men During the Flint, Michigan, Auto Workers' Strike against General Motors, 1937.

and refused to leave until their demands were met, General Motors turned off the heat, blocked entry to the plants and sent police against the picketers outside. Violence erupted. The tide turned when Genora Johnson, a striker's wife, took control of the sound truck and urged other wives to join the picketers. So many women joined that the police had to withdraw. Women also organized food services to supply the strikers, set up a speakers' bureau to present the union's position to the public and formed a Women's Emergency Brigade to take up picket duty. After 44 days, General Motors gave in.

The government encouraged women to work during World War II, prompting six million women to enter the workforce. After the war, most women indicated a desire to stay on the job, but as factories retooled for peacetime work, they fired women, regardless of their skills or seniority.

The Women's Bureau of the United Auto Workers, created in 1944 within the union's war policy division and led by Mildred Jeffrey and Lillian Hatcher, took up this and other issues, such as equal pay for equal work. The bureau pioneered the concept of the "comparable worth" of male and female work, an idea largely ignored until the 1980s. The bureau also discussed seniority rights and child care and protested the expulsion of women from factory jobs reconverted from war production. At the 1946 union convention, the UAW's Council of Women Delegates called for an end to the "female worker" designation that had excluded them from jobs classified as "male." In response, the UAW executive board made the Women's Bureau, a group with strong interracial leadership, a permanent part of its Fair Practices and Anti-Discrimination Department.

Organizing Minority Women Workers

African American women made little labor progress in the immediate postsuffrage era. During the Depression, domestics waited on street corners for potential employers to drive by and offer them work. Some women organized to fight the low wages of these so-called "slave markets," but their organizations did not last long. Through the government, however, a few African American women were able to have an economic impact.

As consultant to the advisory council of the National Youth Administration, Mary Bethune worked to ensure that New Deal programs did not overlook the needs of African Americans. Alice Callis Hunter, the first African American to be elected president of a local League of Women Voters (in the District of Columbia), won appointment to the Consumer Advisory Committee of the Council of Economic Advisors. During World War II, African American and other minority women were able to shift from low-paid or service work into industrial work, which earlier had been closed to them. In 1970, President Nixon chose Elizabeth Koontz, the first African American to lead the National Education Association, to head the U.S. Women's Bureau.

During World War I, thousands of Mexicans had crossed the border to seek work in the United States. By the mid-1920s, they formed the dominant element in the minority populations of the Southwest. Mexican American women worked mostly in domestic or personal service, agriculture or low-skilled industrial jobs, such as sewing, pecan shelling or cigar rolling. In a 1927 strike of pecan

"If I had to give any credit to myself, I would say that I was a darn good organizer."

—Emma Tenayuca

> "We need a leadership endeavoring to develop a trade-union consciousness among Spanish-speaking women."
>
> — Luisa Moreno

shellers and in the massive farm strikes of the 1930s, women played leadership roles.

Emma Tenayuca (b. 1916) took a militant stand against the misery suffered by the Mexican poor of San Antonio, Texas during the Great Depression. Between 1934 and 1948 she supported almost every strike in the city, writing leaflets, visiting homes of strikers and marching with them on the picket lines. In 1936, Tenayuca joined the Workers Alliance, which fought for the right to strike without fear of deportation. They demonstrated for jobs, not relief, and for a minimum wage and hour law. When 12,000 pecan shellers marched out of the factories in 1938, Tenayuca was unanimously elected strike leader.

Luisa Moreno (1906-1992), born in Guatemala and raised in Mexico, organized a Latina garment workers' union called "La Liga de Costureras" in New York City. In 1935, the American Federation of Labor hired her as a professional organizer. She later moved to Florida, where she unionized African American and Latina cigar rollers. She then joined the CIO and in 1938 became affiliated with the United Cannery, Agricultural, Packing, and Allied Workers of America (UCAPAWA-CIO).

From 1938 to 1947, Moreno continued her union work in the Southwest, organizing Mexican farm and food processing workers. About 75 percent of southern California cannery workers were women. Moreno helped them win higher wages and better benefits. During the 1940s, Moreno became the first Latina vice-president of a major U.S. labor union and the first Latina member of the California CIO Council.

Two decades later, in 1962, Jesse Lopez de la Cruz, a farm worker, joined Cesar Chavez in building the United Farm Workers' union. Her focus was on strengthening the Mexican American community by building credit unions and consumer cooperatives. She helped counsel workers seeking citizenship and fought racism in the schools. After mobilizing the grape workers strike of 1966, De La Cruz joined the union's staff and concentrated on organizing women workers.

The Expanding Role of Women at Work

In the 1960s, pressure mounted from women's rights advocates to repeal labor laws that singled out women for special protection. Essential in a time when no workers were protected, such laws now seemed outmoded. After much debate, in 1969 the Equal Employment Opportunity Commission (EEOC), charged with enforcing Title VII of the 1964 Civil Rights Act, which had banned discrimination on the basis of sex, ruled that protective legislation had "ceased to be relevant to our technology or to the expanding role of the female worker in our economy." With this ruling, a strong objection to passing an Equal Rights Amendment was removed.

In 1974, inspired in part by the example of the farm workers, clerical workers formed two organizations, Boston's Nine-to-Five and Women Employed in Chicago. Their protests over the belittling of secretaries' skills and employers' use of secretaries as domestic servants generated countless mini-revolutions in offices across the country. The grassroots movement to increase respect for secretaries, a female-dominated job category, illustrates the union of the women's rights and labor movements.

CHAPTER SIX

WOMEN IN PEACE ACTIVISM AND INTERNATIONAL AFFAIRS

American women were working for peace while they worked for suffrage. In 1887, the Woman's Christian Temperance Union established a Department of Peace and Arbitration. In the 1890s and early 1900s, women participated in movements against imperialistic expansion by world powers, including the United States. Boston pacifist Lucia Mead, for example, actively opposed the U.S. take-over of the Philippines after the Spanish-American war of 1898 and the denial of American citizenship to the country's native people.

Amidst War, Organizing For Peace

Anti-imperialists and suffragists jointly protested the outbreak of world war in 1914. On August 29, 1,500 suffragists dressed in black and carrying a large banner of a dove marched down New York City's Fifth Avenue to the slow beat of a muffled drum. Jane Addams and Carrie Chapman Catt organized a Woman's Peace Party. Lawyer Crystal Eastman, a pioneer in developing worker compensation laws and a militant suffragist, founded a more radical Woman's Peace Party of New York. In November 1915, after President Wilson urged Americans to prepare for war, Eastman and other social reformers formed the American Union Against Militarism, which evolved later into the American Civil Liberties Union (ACLU).

In 1915, industrial physician Alice Hamilton and social worker Jane Addams attended an International Congress of Women at The Hague that urged continuous mediation among the belligerent states and an armistice. A Second International Congress of Women in Zurich in 1919 led to the founding of the Women's International League for Peace and Freedom (WILPF). This group issued the first criticisms of the Versailles Treaty and emphasized the connection between war and the economic and racial oppression that accompanies imperialism. The League vigorously opposed the U.S. marine occupations of Haiti (1915-1934) and Nicaragua (1912-1925 and 1926-1933).

After the war, the WILPF mounted a campaign against militarism, working closely with the League of Women Voters (LWV), the Women's Joint Congressional Committee and the Daughters of the American Revolution (DAR). This campaign gave rise to a vicious attack from the U.S. Department of War. In 1923, Brigadier General Amos A. Fries, head of the department's Chemical Warfare Department, circulated a copy of a "spider web" chart showing the interconnected activities of presumed "radical" women's societies and church groups. The chart linked Jane Addams, the WILPF and even the DAR with communism.

In 1925, former suffragist and League of Women Voters founder Carrie Chapman Catt organized the Committee on the Cause and Cure of War (CCCW), a coalition of 11 major women's organizations. The group hoped to increase world understanding of the causes of war and devise ways to stop it. In annual conferences, "Marathon Round Tables" and extension courses, it promoted the development of negotiation and arbitration systems. It also trained a cadre of female foreign policy experts, some of whom entered government in the 1930s.

Jeannette Rankin, the Montana suffragist and social reformer who in 1916 won election as the first woman member of the U.S. Congress, became a noted peace activist. After one term in the House of Representatives, she ran for the Senate but lost. She then became a WILPF field secretary and board member. The Georgia Peace Society, which Rankin founded in 1928 after moving to Athens, Georgia, served as the base of her peace operations until its demise on the eve of World War II. She worked for ten years as Washington lobbyist and field organizer for the National Council for the Prevention of War. Elected to Congress a second time, she cast the only vote against U.S. entry into World War II, a vote that cost her reelection. Over her remaining years, Rankin opposed Cold War policies and American domination of underdeveloped countries.

Anger over the rejection of the League of Nations by the U.S. Congress fueled much of women's activism in international affairs after suffrage. Led by Maud Wood Park, League of Women Voters' president and chair of the World Court subcommittee of the Women's Joint Congressional Committee, women launched a campaign to urge Congress to approve U.S. participation in a World Court. Despite close cooperation with prominent supporters in the legal community, the campaign failed. The vote in January 1935 fell seven votes short of the two-thirds required for ratification.

LWV activist Ruth Morgan led a women's movement in favor of the Kellogg-Briand Pact, negotiated in 1928 between U.S. Secretary of State Frank Kellogg and French Foreign Minister Aristide Briand. The treaty was originally conceived to outlaw war between the two countries. To avoid the appearance of a Franco-American alliance, Kellogg proposed that the pact renounce war "as an instrument of foreign policy." Any nation could sign such a pact. Using the organizations of the nine groups in the CCCW coalition, Morgan showered Washington with letters, delegations and copies of resolutions passed at public meetings. This outpouring of support was decisive in winning congressional approval of the pact, 85 to 1.

Carter Glass of Virginia dubbed Kellogg-Briand a "worthless, but perfectly harmless peace treaty." As one historian has said, however, for CCCW members it was "the quintessential expression of their moral vision applied to foreign policy." Judge Florence Allen, a WILPF member, compared the treaty to laws that make murder a crime: such laws do not eliminate murder but they do establish a social belief and allow its perpetrators to be punished.

The WILPF attracted Emily Greene Balch (1867-1961), a former settlement worker who taught economics at Wellesley College. Involved in many reform campaigns of the era, she served on the first commission on minimum wages for women in Massachusetts and cofounded and presided over the Boston Women's Trade Union League. During World War I, Balch participated in the 1915 international women's peace movement. She became increasingly radical, writing against the war, espionage legislation, the draft, and the attacks on the civil liberties of conscientious objectors and the foreign-born. In 1919, Wellesley did not renew Balch's contract.

Balch became secretary-treasurer of the WILPF in Geneva. After 1922 she remained with WILPF as a volunteer, trying to hold the group together despite political disagreements among its members. She published a book on conditions in Haiti *(Occupied Haiti,* 1927) and supported Kellogg-Briand. She urged President Hoover to impose sanctions on Japan for its invasion of Manchuria in 1931, and in the 1930s pressed for the reception of refugees from Nazi persecution. She supported the U.S. declaration of war against Japan after Pearl Harbor but urged WILPF members to help Japanese-Americans being sent to internment camps. In 1946, Balch became the second woman to win the Nobel Peace Prize (Jane Addams was the first, in 1933), a prize that also recognized the work of the WILPF.

As the events leading toward a second world war escalated, women set aside their peace efforts. The CCCW became the "Women's Action Committee for Victory and Lasting Peace."

The WILPF, suffering from internal divisions and a reputation of being sympathetic to communism, settled on neutrality. In 1941, the organization acknowledged the fact of war, worked to protect civil liberties and plan for the peace, and protested the relocation of Japanese-Americans.

After World War I, women who had learned about international affairs through women's peace activism began to play formal roles in government service. Mary Woolley (1863-1947), president of Mount Holyoke College (1900-1937), served also as president of the American Association of University Women (AAUW) from 1927 to 1933 and then as head of its international committee. Acceding to pressure from women's organizations, President Hoover appointed her a delegate to the 1932 Geneva Conference on Reduction and Limitation of Armaments. Woolley was the first woman to represent the United States at an important diplomatic conference.

Woolley worked for peace and disarmament throughout the 1930s and after World War II. She organized the Committee on the Participation of Women in Post-War Policy (later, Women in World Affairs). Determined to get more women appointed to international organizations and conferences, she found out when appointments were open, solicited names of potential women appointees and organized letter-writing campaigns on behalf of the candidates. Woolley included African Americans in this process, soliciting a representative of the National Council of Negro Women for her organization's executive board and recommending black women for openings in government agencies.

Eleanor Roosevelt was perhaps the most prominent woman

"*When will our consciences grow so tender that we will act to prevent human misery rather than avenge it?*"

—Eleanor Roosevelt

in international affairs after World War II. In 1945, President Truman appointed her to the first U.S. delegation to the United Nations. The following year, Truman asked Roosevelt to be the American delegate to the U.N. Human Rights Commission, charged with drafting an international bill of rights. Negotiating a Declaration of Human Rights took her three years. Rising Cold War tensions and international sensibilities taxed her parliamentary and diplomatic skills. When the General Assembly passed the Declaration on December 10, 1948, delegates rose in unison to applaud Roosevelt's stunning work.

During the Cold War, women again provided much of the grassroots support for peace activism. Prominent women's organizations, including the League of Women Voters, the American Association of University Women, the National Council of Jewish Women, the YWCA, the National Federation of Business and Professional Women's Clubs, and the Women's Trade Union League, all supported the United Nations and encouraged U.S. support for international peacekeeping efforts.

The rise of McCarthyism put a damper on some of this activity. When Cold War anticommunist crusaders began calling the United Nations a "communist plot" for world domination, mainstream women's organizations pulled back on their liberal international policies. McCarthyism affected even organizations known for their patriotism. After World War II, Girl Scouts-USA put a renewed emphasis on international friendship and "world citizenship." A Florida television newscaster attacked the 1953 Girl Scout handbook for its praise of the UN, and the Illinois American Legion terminated its support of Girl Scouting because the handbook endorsed "world" over American citizenship. These attacks forced the Girl Scouts to tone down internationalism in subsequent editions.

In 1954, in response to the climate of fear and demagoguery, the League of Women Voters launched a "Freedom Agenda" project to remind Americans of the importance of maintaining individual constitutional liberties. The nationwide project, which eventually included a number of distinguished academics and many other organizations, set up hundreds of local discussion meetings to underscore the enduring meaning of such issues as freedom of speech and expression. Although attacked by the right wing, the League refused to disavow the project and eventually saw the tide turn against the philosophy and tactics of McCarthyism.

The Jeannette Rankin Brigade Protests the Vietnam War on Capitol Hill, 1968.

A Unique Voice

Men dominated the chief mixed-sex pacifist organizations of the Cold War era, such as the American Friends Service Committee and the Fellowship of Reconciliation. During the 1960s, however, women began to articulate a unique position. In 1961, Dagmar Wilson led women active in the Committee for a SANE Nuclear Policy to found the Women's Strike for Peace (WSP). A grassroots organization consisting of "housewives," the group protested the continued atmospheric testing of nuclear weapons and the fall-out of Strontium 90 into the food chain and eventually into mothers' milk.

On November 1, 1961, as a cloud of radioactive dust from a Soviet test floated across the United States, the WSP called for a one-day "strike" of mothers. On that day, an estimated 50,000 women left their jobs and homes to lobby government officials. "End the Arms Race, Not the Human Race," their banners cried: "Not Our Sons, Not Your Sons, Not Their Sons."

Over the next year, 60 local WSP chapters formed. In December 1962, the House Un-American Activities Committee called in the organization for investigation. Refusing to be intimidated, grandmothers and mothers with children on their hips cheered, booed and gave bouquets to witnesses, in general refusing to conform to expectations of "housewifely" behavior.

As the Vietnam War escalated, the WSP picketed draft offices and began lobbying Congress to end American participation, led by Bella Abzug, who in 1971 would become a member of Congress from New York. The organization addressed NATO meetings in Geneva and in 1969 sent a delegation to Hanoi to meet with North Vietnamese women. The WSP helped create the rising public opinion in favor of a nuclear test ban, an end to the draft and the withdrawal of U.S. troops from Vietnam.

On January 15, 1968, a "Jeannette Rankin Brigade," a coalition of pacifists, anti-war students and radicals, demonstrated against the Vietnam war in Washington, DC. On that day, the link between the woman suffrage campaign and women's long history of peace activism was reforged.

CONCLUSION

DOES WOMEN'S PARTICIPATION IN POLITICS COUNT?

Women have engaged in politics in many different ways since suffrage. They formed and joined voluntary associations, and some rose to community leadership positions. They participated in political parties, in the early days mostly from the sidelines but later in more important advisory posts and eventually as party officers. As women's professional and political footholds grew more secure, they sought and won appointive office. They ran for elective office, losing most races at the start but later winning judicial, legislative and—at local and state levels—executive posts.

Women followed all of these routes to power. Changing life circumstances, such as marriage, childrearing or career needs, often determined the path they chose. Of course, opportunity also was a factor. Most political women did not initially choose politics as a career. Usually, they gained political experience first through grassroots volunteer work or a job. Someone in power (more often than not, a man) noted their accomplishments, opened a door to greater responsibility and urged them to walk through it.

Women's activism has had appreciable results. American men have enjoyed, and still enjoy, the preponderance of power in political and public affairs, but women always have been there in some capacity and their presence has made a difference. Still, most histories of American political life continue to empha-

size male leadership. And no wonder. As of the mid-1990s, all U.S. presidents, the most powerful members of Congress and government officials, and the leaders of most of the country's mixed-sex voluntary associations have been men.

Since most women's activism has centered on grassroots organizing, the task of reconstructing women's influence has been too tedious and difficult to attract many historians. Even when women have held important party or policy posts, historians have rarely paid much attention to them. In part, this is because documentation of their activities is hard to come by. Some women did not consider their actions important enough to preserve a record. The papers of others have been lost, discarded or buried in family collections or government archives that often are difficult to access. A persistent and determined hand can often find records of these women, but without informed interpretation, their meaning will not be understood.

Does it matter if women get credit in history for their grassroots organizing and the groundwork they laid for important policy decisions? Yes. Women's historical invisibility has perpetuated the view that women are unsuited for leadership. A more balanced history should change this view and help open more opportunities for women.

Over time, scholars of women's history have unearthed and worked to preserve the stories of women's important roles in the nation's public affairs. Few of those stories entered the mainstream, however, and succeeding generations had to discover them anew. The history of women should be an integral part of the history easily available to all Americans, male and female alike, and especially to young people. Only with full knowledge and appreciation of the past contributions made by women and men from all parts of our society can we move forward to build on their achievements together.

Bibliography

Background

Abramovitz, Mimi. *Regulating the Lives of Women: Social Welfare Policy from Colonial Times to the Present* (1988).

Chafe, William H. *The Paradox of Change: American Women in the 20th Century* (1992).

Evans, Sara M. *Born for Liberty: A History of Women in America* (1989).

Flexner, Eleanor. *Century of Struggle: The Woman's Rights Movement in America* (1975).

Giddings, Paula. *When and Where I Enter: The Impact of Black Women on Race and Sex in America* (1984).

Hosokawa, Bill. *The Japanese American Citizens League: In Quest of Justice* (1982).

Matthews, Glenna. *The Rise of Public Woman: Woman's Power and Woman's Place in the U.S., 1630-1970* (1992).

Muncy, Robyn. *Creating a Female Dominion in American Reform, 1890-1935* (1991).

Scott, Anne Firor. *Natural Allies: Women's Associations in American History* (1992).

Young, Louise M. *In the Public Interest: The League of Women Voters, 1920-1970* (1989).

Between The Wars

Alonso, Harriet Hyman. *Peace As a Women's Issue: A History of the U.S. Movement for World Peace and Women's Rights* (1993).

Becker, Susan D. *The Origins of the Equal Rights Amendment: American Feminism Between the Wars* (1981).

Cott, Nancy F. *The Grounding of Modern Feminism* (1987).

Dye, Nancy Schrom. *As Equals & As Sisters: Feminism, Unionism, and the Women's Trade Union League of New York* (1980).

Gordon, Felice D. *After Winning: The Legacy of the New Jersey Suffragists, 1920-1947* (1986).

Lemons, J. Stanley. *The Woman Citizen: Social Feminism in the 1920s* (1975).

Ruiz, Vicki L. *Cannery Women, Cannery Lives: Mexican Women, Unionization, and the California Food Processing Industry, 1930-1950* (1987).

Scharf, Lois and Joan Jensen, eds. *Decades of Discontent: The Women's Movement, 1920-1940* (1983).

Ware, Susan. *Beyond Suffrage: Women in the New Deal* (1981).

After World War I

Evans, Sara. *Personal Politics: The Roots of Women's Liberation in the Civil Rights Movement and the New Left* (1979).

Crawford, Vicki L., Jacqueline Anne Rouse, and Barbara Woods, eds. *Women in the Civil Rights Movement: Trailblazers & Torchbearers, 1941-1965* (1990).

Freeman, Jo. *The Politics of Women's Liberation* (1975).

Harrison, Cynthia. *On Account of Sex: The Politics of Women's Issues 1945-1968* (1989).

Hartmann, Susan M. *From Margin to Mainstream: American Women and Politics Since 1960* (1989).

Hoff-Wilson, Joan, ed. *Rights of Passage: The Past and Future of the ERA* (1986).

Linden-Ward, Blanche and Carol Hurd Green. *American Women in the 1960s: Changing the Future* (1993).

Lynn, Susan. *Progressive Women in Conservative Times: Racial Justice, Peace, and Feminism, 1945 to the 1960s* (1992).

Rupp, Leila J. and Verta Taylor. *Survival in the Doldrums: The American Women's Rights Movement, 1945 to the 1960s* (1987).

Swerdlow, Amy. *Women Strike for Peace: Traditional Motherhood and Radical Politics in the 1960s* (1993).

Autobiographies, Biographies, and Memoirs

Cook, Blanche Wiesen. *Eleanor Roosevelt* (1992).

Durr, Virginia Foster. *Outside the Magic Circle: The Autobiography of Virginia Foster Durr* (1985).

Hall, Jacquelyn Dowd. *Revolt Against Chivalry: Jessie Daniel Ames and the Women's Campaign Against Lynching* (1979).

Irwin, Inez Haynes. *The Story of Alice Paul* (repr., 1977).

Martin, George F. *Madame Secretary: Frances Perkins* (1976).

Miller, Kristie. *Ruth Hanna McCormick, A Life in Politics 1880-1944* (1992).

Murray, Pauli. *Autobiography of a Black Activist, Feminist, Lawyer, Priest, and Poet* (1989).

Park, Maud Wood. *Front Door Lobby* (1960).

Peck, Mary G. *Carrie Chapman Catt: A Biography* (1944).

Perry, Elisabeth I. *Belle Moskowitz: Feminine Politics and the Exercise of Power in the Age of Alfred E. Smith* (1987).

Robinson, Jo Ann Gibson. *The Montgomery Bus Boycott and the Women Who Started It* (1987).

Sklar, Kathryn Kish. *Florence Kelley and the Nation's Work: The Rise of Women's Political Culture, 1830-1900* (1995).

Scobie, Ingrid Winther. *Center Stage: A Biography of Helen Gahagan Douglas, 1900-1980* (1992).

Ware, Susan. *Partner and I: Molly Dewson, Feminism, and New Deal Politics* (1987).

Author's Note

Elisabeth Israels Perry directs the Graduate Program in Women's History at Sarah Lawrence College in Bronxville, New York. She taught U.S. women's history at Vanderbilt University from 1985-1993, with a year as Daniel M. Lyons Visiting Professor in U.S. History at Brooklyn College-City University of New York (1991-1992). Her books include *Belle Moskowitz: Feminine Politics and the Exercise of Power in the Age of Alfred E. Smith* (1987); *The Challenge of Feminist Biography: Writing the Lives of Modern American Women* (1992), which she coedited; and *America: Pathways to the Present* (1994), which she coauthored. Perry received her Ph.D. in history from the University of California at Los Angeles.

The author is grateful to the members of the Advisory Committee of the League of Women Voters Education Fund history project who offered constructive comments on the first draft of this publication. She would also like to thank Lewis Perry, Irma Commanday Bauman, Kathryn Kish Sklar, and Susan Ware for their many helpful suggestions, and acknowledge the aid of Kris Ann Cappelluti, her research assistant.